Discipline Your Way to Success

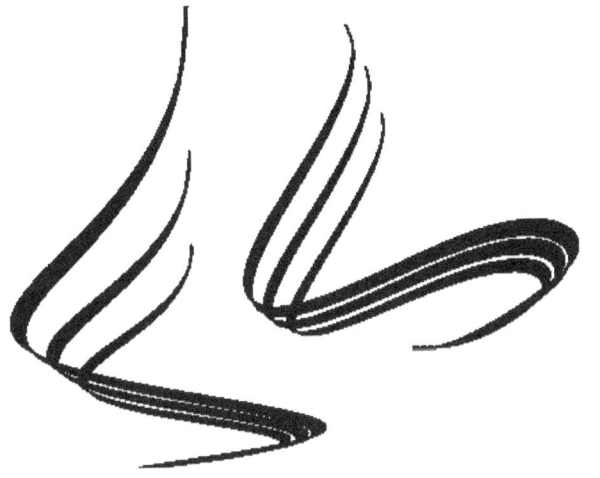

Discipline Your Way to Success

The Definitive Guide to Success Through Self-Discipline

Why Self-Discipline is Crucial to Your Success Story and How to Take Control Over Your Thoughts and Actions

Your Path to Success: A Five Part Series

Chase Andrews

Copyright © 2017 by Chase Andrews

All rights reserved. No part of this publication may be reproduced, distributed, or transmitted in any form or by any means, including photocopying, recording, or other electronic or mechanical methods, without the prior written permission of the publisher, except in the case of brief quotations embodied in critical reviews and certain other noncommercial uses permitted by copyright law. For permission requests, write to the publisher, addressed "Attention: Permissions Coordinator," at the address below.

Chase Andrews

chaseandrews@thepassiveincomemachine.com

www.thepassiveincomemachine.com

Make sure to check out the rest of the books in this series:

Fail Your Way to Success: The Definitive Guide to Failing Forward and Learning How to Extract the Greatness Within - Why Failing is an Integral Part of Success and Why You Should Never Fear it

https://www.amazon.com/dp/B0738WDK6W

Meditate Your Way to Success: The Definitive Guide to Mindfulness, Focus and Meditation - How Meditation is an Integral Part of Success and Why You Should Get Started Now

https://www.amazon.com/dp/B073ZMCHQJ

Ask Your Way to Success: The Definitive Guide to Success Through Asking - How to Transform Your Life by Learning the Art of Asking

https://www.amazon.com/dp/B074CJPFMH

Believe Your Way to Success: The Definitive Guide to Believing and Your Path to Success How Believing Takes You from Where You are to Where You Want to Be

https://www.amazon.com/dp/B0747N14KF

This book is dedicated to those of you who can feel the greatness within you, but can't figure out how to capture it.

You are all you need. Everything you need to be great is already within you. You just need to know master your thoughts, your mind, and your actions. This book, and this series, reveals to you exactly how to do that.

This book is dedicated to your future self. The future version of you that has a huge positive impact on the world and leaves it much better than how you found it.

Contents

Prologue
- Discipline's Place in the Grand Scheme of Success

Preface
- Four Truths of Success

Introduction

Chapter 1 What it Means to Be Human
- Forces
- Simile of the Raft
- Imaginary Forces
- Right and Wrong
- Takeaway

Chapter 2 Dominant Personality
- Actions and Reactions

Chapter 3 Purpose
- Dual Purpose Life
- Greatness is Your Purpose
- Is Greatness Not for Everyone?

Chapter 4 An Introduction to Discipline
- Filial Discipline
- Societal Discipline
- Personal Discipline
- Carrot and Stick
- The Arc of Discipline
- The Importance of Discipline

    The Insidious Nature of Indiscipline

    Why Does the Body Not Want to Act?

Chapter 5 Overcoming Resistance to Action

Chapter 6 Face to Face With Discipline

    Thoughts

    Actions

    Discipline Flows from Focus

Chapter 7 How to Invoke Discipline

    Focus

    Energy Economics

    Behavioral Change

Chapter 8 Theory vs. Practice

    Exercises

    Fasting

    Muscle Building

Conclusion

Epilogue

Prologue

This is the second book of a five-part series on success. While you should read all five to get a holistic understanding of success, you don't need to read them in sequence. So, if this is your first book in the series - strap in, it's going to be a wild ride.

Discipline's Place in the Grand Scheme of Success

With the understanding of these four areas which are touched on and explained in different volumes of the series, you will get to understand yourself and how these factors have shaped you across time. With that understanding, you can then begin to lay the new foundation that consists of the five following elements:

The first is the ability to understand failure, and how failure can lead to success.

The second is to recognize and internalize discipline so that when your inspiration demands shifting into high gear and bringing forth massive action, your body will do as you mind commands. The first two books set the stage for success and what it means, and why you shouldn't short-change yourself as to the height of your success.

The third is the power of meditation that you need to understand your place and purpose in the world so that you can go on to leverage who you are and make greatness bear fruit.

The fourth is that you must understand the role of asking and how asking for what you want does not start and stop at your lip but vibrates within the silence of your meditation. The fourth element needed is the ability to ask and a strong grasp of what to ask for. People are often astounded by how simple the notion of asking really is. We sometimes choose not to ask, because subconsciously we are not ready for success, or we fear it. If you can't ask for success, then it should occur to you that there is some form of baggage that you need to jettison and that can be taken care of by means of meditation and reflection. Asking is an art that you need to internalize. As simple as it sounds, many of you lose the ability and the inclination to ask for what you want. Asking is both the start of your journey and the expansion of it. Whatever you ask for, the Universe will grant.

Finally, there is the element of belief. You need to believe that anything and everything is possible. You need to believe that what you will embark on will yield a positive result in the making of your success and the reaching of your greatness.

To this end, we have laid out five titles in this success series.

   i. Fail Your Way to Success
   ii. Discipline Your Way to Success
   iii. Meditate Your Way to Success
   iv. Ask Your Way to Success
   v. Believe Your Way to Success

A word of advice, if I may:

This series will bear optimum results when approached with an open mind. To touch the secrets the material presents in its entirety, you will have to lay assault on it multiple times, reflect on its meaning, and then attack it once again. You will be surprised to see how the same lines can have a deeper impact each subsequent time you come at it until you get to a point that the information becomes fluid and your own truth emerges from it.

***

Preface

Before Chuck Yeager and the Bell X-1 he was flying broke the sound barrier, the world of aviation was strongly steeped in the belief and certainty that man could not fly faster than the speed of sound. They were so certain, that it eventually came to be known as a barrier - the sound barrier. The belief among professionals that it could not be done was unanimous. Aerodynamicists said it was impossible to predict airflow behind a shock wave. Structural engineers could not be certain if the aircraft could withstand the forces; and propulsion engineers were convinced that they couldn't get engines to produce the significant amount of thrust needed to take the vehicle past the huge spike in drag that happens around Mach 1. Aircraft design methodology, in and of itself, was unable to rise to the challenge.

Nothing can be solved if you only search for the solution in the same plane as the problem. It is a fundamental truth in all things. Even Einstein believed that. To solve something, you have to conquer it by getting above it. It's like when Newton tried to solve the calculations to predict the path of Halley's Comet and when he tried to understand gravity. He couldn't just solve it where he stood; he had to go to a whole new level to do it. And he did - he developed a whole new branch of mathematics - calculus, to be able to solve these problems of gravity and motion. So in the same way, engineers on both sides of the Atlantic decided to get on top of the design problems of aircraft design and reinvent the way they looked at flight.

It was in the early 1940s; there was a sudden will - a sudden desire and the concerted effort fueled by military concerns, to develop a new generation of aircraft based on new design philosophies. They wanted to do more than the previous generations could. The discipline to climb out of what was comfortable and commonly known and search for new ideas resulted in the X-plane program and the massive action that went into it culminated in accumulation of large amounts of data that eventually changed the way we view manned flight.

One of the notable outcomes of the X-plane program was the eventual ability to break the sound barrier. Once that barrier was broken, we began to design planes that regularly reached speeds of four, five and even six times the speed of sound. Chuck Yeager and the X-plane team had redefined the definition of success within the aviation world, pushed the boundaries of contemporary belief, and flew into greatness.

It took a bold leap forward. One that was pure inspiration, coupled with the discipline to execute ideas that had no basis in experience. The same thing was done when JFK committed the country to put a man on the moon. It was a huge goal that required tremendous effort and strict discipline on a national scale. But the outcome was one of greatness, and it changed the world forever. It changed America forever.

Today the Bell X-1, as well the Command Module of the Apollo 11 Mission hang in the Smithsonian Air and Space Museum in Washington DC, a symbol not just of vehicles that vanquished engineering barriers, but as reminders that barriers in our mind can be torn down by inspiration and discipline.

The homage we pay Yeager and the X-1 are not about man's ability to breach Mach 1, because, since then, countless men and women around the world, even civilians aboard the Concord, have breached that once elusive barrier. Instead, we celebrate Yeager for being the face of inspiration, intelligence, and discipline in removing the barrier within our minds and in the minds of the generations to come that something was once impossible. Yeager personifies the entire Herculean effort of the X-plane program that enabled man to conquer the different barriers of flight.

The most significant barrier we face is not the one in physical reality; it's the imaginary one within us. But even though that barrier is imaginary, it seems real enough to us, and daunting enough to scare us into inaction. That path to eventual greatness starts with the tearing down of walls and barriers we construct in our head. To do that we need inspiration. Then we need discipline to move that inspiration from the realm of the intangible to the realm of the physical. Random thought and willed cogitation, in itself, are not enough; we need more. That something more is divine inspiration.

From divine inspiration of things we have never seen before, we need to convert that to something we can use in this world of physical manifestation. To figure that out we use our mind, our intellect, our ability to learn, and ability to apply what we know to different things - all the abilities of the brain

In a nutshell, success can be described as the ability to navigate the arc that goes from ideas born of inspiration, made viable by cogitation, and made real by perspiration. It's about making things and moving them with your hands or building things until each successive event of success comes flying at you in rapid sequence and you reach the level of greatness you were born to achieve.

That's what you can do for yourself and what you must do by yourself. You need to redefine your view of success, because you are short-changing yourself if your definition of success doesn't bring you closer to greatness.

There is a Bill Gates, a Thomas Edison, a Steve Jobs, a Henry Ford, a Chuck Yeager, or a Muhammad Ali, in all of us. But it never surfaces because we are too scared to see it and too afraid to move on it. Success takes hard work, takes fine tuning of our abilities, and uncommon mindsets. Success takes change - from who we are to who we want to be, and change brings about two things: fear and resistance. Fear because we are always afraid of the unknown, and resistance because we never want to let go of what we are certain of. Nothing causes us to stop achieving. We do that to ourselves. Reversing that is what discipline is for.

If you want to be successful, you have to break old forms and unproductive habits; to help you get to that point, this series on success is laid out in five books. One book for each element details why you need to invoke it and sharpen it until it is at peak performance within you. You don't just learn these elements, you become them.

If you are not getting into a rhythm of success after success, then there is a block between one of the three stages. If you are not coming up with the ideas then it's an inspiration problem. If you are not translating your inspiration into viable plans, then it's a thinking problem. If you're not converting viable plans into action, then it's a discipline problem.

Four Truths of Success

The first thing you need to do is cast off your notion of success, especially if your notion is defined and molded by the rewards you see enjoyed by those you think are successful. Look again. You need to scrub your mind of any notion that links reward and success. Mahatma Gandhi was highly accomplished and achieved greatness during his lifetime (By the way, Mahatma is not his first name - his full name is Mohandas Karamchand Gandhi. Mahatma, in Hindi/Sanskrit, just means Great Soul - a term ascribing greatness to a mortal). His greatness was achieved not by the pursuit and achievement of economic wealth, but by nobler, altruistic means. Rewards are not the same thing as success.

The second thing you should know is that greatness that follows a string of successes can only come from truly inspired visions that are not possible to arrive at by mere mental cogitation alone. Mental cogitation merely defines a plan to take that brilliant fruit of inspiration and make it real. You need to be at one and at peace with the universe to be able to understand your vision and to have visions that will guide your hand to succeed.

The third thing that you must come to terms with is that your limitations are not permanent. Limitations are not terminal. Limitations are stumbling blocks, and stumbling blocks are either something you trip over or something you use to climb higher. So, just as blocks are just blocks and you can use them to trip you or raise you, so are limitations there to trip you or enhance you.

The fourth is that you must understand fear and face it. You need to understand that fear has its purpose and is the vestige of a binary response system that was needed to keep the balance of predator and prey. On top of the binary response to fear, fight or flight, our fear profile becomes more sophisticated as we develop higher brain function. Now, we define fear as a physiological condition that comes about in response to real or imagined stimuli that could result in one, or more hazards. Typically, achieving success always seems to demand that one or more of these hazards be challenged when we set ourselves on the path to success. For this reason, most people back off and rather take on a mediocre life.

Introduction

As a young teenager, I used to find myself constantly in trouble. My parents had a hard time telling me to do something and having reasonable expectations that it would get done. The funny thing is that they weren't alone. I had the same problem. A lot of the things I told myself to do, seemed to not get done either. There seemed to be a bit of a disconnect between what I knew needed to happen, and what I actually made happen.

It turns out that there was a missing element in the process that goes from deciding to do something, and actually doing it. You can motivate yourself all you want, you can reward yourself upon a task's completion to the nth degree, or you can be praised for your past efforts, but if you are missing this one crucial bridge, then nothing is going to move from intangible inspiration to tangible achievement.

That element that's missing in those of us who are inspired to move the world but can't seem to move a finger is the element of discipline. Discipline is a funny thing. It is wholly misinterpreted as a child and utterly misunderstood as an adult. As children, we think of discipline as the word that surfaces just before we are faced with unpleasant tasks. As adults, we think of self-discipline as a chore yet invoke the rule of discipline over our wards.

Discipline is much simpler than extreme definitions of fealty or difficulty. Discipline is about our mind's ability to take control of our body's impulses and desires and direct our actions towards the goals our mind has set while overriding the body's reason for inaction or insufficient action. Without discipline, we are unable to muster the set of forces required to take what inspiration has given us and mold it into what can move the world.

But under the spotlight of success, discipline needs to become something more powerful altogether. Under the spotlight of success, we can no longer look at discipline in filial or interpersonal relationships. We need to look at discipline intrapersonally - within ourselves. The kind I never had as a kid - knowing what to do but never having the will (or the discipline) to do it.

You need to take the time to understand the element of discipline, differentiate what it is and what it's not, and stare deeply into the powers that discipline can unlock within you once you understand its secrets. The best way to apply discipline is to internalize it - make it a part of you, and to do so, you have to first acknowledge its existence and the degree it exists within you. You have to understand its deficit, and you have to understand its limits.

We are not born with any form of discipline because it initially never occurs to us that we can do something different than what our body instructs. That's one of the reasons kids do things that may seem inappropriate. Entrepreneurs are never born with it either; they substitute discipline for passion and the rush they get from seeing incremental objectives materializing in their hands. It's like a sculptor seeing his craft come to life in his hands. This can be dangerous too, because the flame of passion can burn out, and when it does, you are left crippled by the inability to move yourself because you have not been developing your discipline.

Commercial motivational outlets promote the hacking of minds in place of discipline. Discipline is discipline; you don't get it by making believe that you are being chased by a tiger to run faster. You don't imagine doom, to instigate action. You don't play on your fears to illicit results. All these hacks work for a while and give you a couple of hits here and there. But then, before you know it, they stop working because your subconscious is not stupid. It catches on, and when it does, it wises up to your act. Don't go down this road. Instead, spend your time and resources building up your discipline. Be straight with yourself and get your conscious and subconscious to work together rather than working against each other.

***

Chapter 1 What it Means to Be Human

Success is a journey that goes from your current self to a better version of you, able to do things that you once thought impossible. Taking your bike down to the corner store is not a success, but taking your bike down a double black diamond trail for the first time would constitute a success. The difference is your ability in handling the terrain where any version of yourself would be able to handle the ride to the corner, but a stronger, more athletic version of you is needed to make it down the trail.

Being human is a complicated endeavor. There are so many forces, some in opposition, acting on us constantly. We have environmental forces that pervade us, psychological forces that sway us, social forces that influence us, and even economic forces that drive us. We are never just the result of one of these forces, we are typically an amalgam of all, and each changes one day to the next, just like the slope of a double black diamond.

Forces

All those forces aside, we have two more forces that mean the most to us. They mean the most because they are within us. These two internal forces are usually improperly named, and throughout the ages, many writers and theologians have called it one or the other. Some have even gone as far as to call one an angel and the other a demon. Cartoons mimic this by putting a cherub on one shoulder while putting a devil on the other - each whispering in your ear to do their bidding.

The only thing correct about that visual is that we, as humans, are slave to these forces. Our mistakes in life and our shortcomings in character are typically rooted in this dichotomy of self. There is a rational explanation for the two sides, one that does not rely on religious or mythical interpretations. These are the parts of you that you have to come to know and understand if you are to have a shot at being successful.

One of these two parts dictates actions that authors like Dante Alighieri describe in his Divine Comedy as the seven stages of hell. Christians call it the seven deadly sins. We can call it whatever we like, but it is the basic instinct of our primal self in full display. The seven deadly sins are gluttony, lust, envy, wrath, sloth, pride, and greed. We are told that when we do not control the devil within us from committing any one of these sins, we are doomed to hell.

The part of us that makes us do these things is really the primal and ancient part of us that got us through turbulent times of pre-civilization. Without the skills of greed, we would not have been able to go out and forage for food, so that we have stores when winter comes. Without envy, we would not have been able to mimic what others have done and thereby better ourselves. Without wrath, we would not have been able to spark defensive mechanisms and protect ourselves and our families. Without sloth, we would not have been able to rest and recuperate. Without lust, we would not have been able to expand the species and prolong it. Of course, I am oversimplifying - but not by a stretch. For each of those 'sins' there was a viable reason for its existence and how, at one time, it worked in our favor.

When you fast forward a couple of millennia, you find that none of those actions seem appropriate; and if you take part in any of those acts, the long-term repercussions are more detrimental than beneficial. So, in the long term, there are negative consequences to unmitigated acts sparked by our primal instincts.

As civilizations rose from the deserts and humans began to understand the benefits of communities and shared resources, new norms of behavior replaced the old. New social contracts took hold, forcing individuals to do things differently. These acts were defined by the different forces I mentioned earlier - social, economic, and so on. Consequences for non-compliance of living in civilizations and in communities were harsh and ranged from the loss of limbs to loss of life to outright banishment - all severe by any standard. In time, the repercussions forced individuals in line, and eventually, life changed at a fundamental level.

As we developed under the social forces of this new format of shared living, our brains improved and evolved with the better nutrition standards, lesser survival stresses from the previous hunter-gatherer models of living, then the farming and bartering models, to the current monetary supply and demand commodity economies we have now, where there are multiple degrees of separation from product genesis to product consumption. Greed, a natural instinct to want more, which once served its purpose, no longer manifests in the same way. Once a desired trait, greed, in today's context, has become socially unacceptable.

In the same way that we can visualize greed and its fall from grace, we can visualize each of the remaining six of the seven deadly sins. Placing whatever religious connotations aside, and looking at merely the practicality of the matter, you will begin to understand that the seven vices were once seven angels. But because humanity has evolved, humanity has marched forward and civilizations have become what they are. What was once necessary has now become more than just unnecessary; it has become counterproductive and thus evil.

Simile of the Raft

There is a Buddhist sutra (Buddha's teaching) that is very interesting and relevant to this discussion. It is known as the Simile of the Raft. It tells a tale of a man walking in the forest, on the side of a river that's filled with dangers. He comes upon the river and sees that the other side is safe and he desires to cross this river. The problem is that he is unable to swim or walk across and needs a raft. There isn't one in sight. But there are enough branches and leaves and prop roots. The man uses all he can find and builds a raft using much effort and time. When it is finally ready, this effort of his back and work of his hands delivers him safely across the river to the safer side. When he gets to the other side, he knows that his journey takes him inland and not along the river. But he has a problem. What does he now do with this raft that he spent tremendous effort and toil building? Should he find a way of dragging it along, lift it over his head, or should he just let it be?

Think about that for a while and let it sink in.

Even though it may seem like we left something behind, we really haven't. Once we have done something, it remains a part of us. That raft may have floated downstream, someone else may have been able to use it, or it may even have gradually disintegrated. But the knowledge he gained while building it, the confidence he gets from knowing he can do it, and even the ability to do it better the next time will never leave him - he will always carry that with him. Just as Heraclitus once said, "No man ever steps in the same river twice, for it is not the same river, and he is not the same man".

But we have to leave things behind once they have served its purpose, and you have to unburden your shoulders and unburden your mind from its weight and its memory so that you can go on to the next state of being. Just as the Apollo rockets and the space shuttle jettison their stage one and two rockets as they ascend toward space; you have the discipline to free yourself of anchors as you move from one state to the next.

The man in the simile of the raft was changed by his experience - changed for the better, and will always remain that way, and in that way, he is the same as the river - which with each drop of water that flows in it makes it different.

In that exact same way, we may not act and behave at the impulse of the forces that got us here. We may have cast aside its influence in how we act. But it is within us. Our desires and temptations are exactly these forces that carried us over time and space. Today, we need the more contemporary part of our brain. We need our logic, and we need to temper our instincts so that we can navigate our purpose to live life. Remember, our supreme purpose is to live life. In the past, we used our primal instincts and it served us well. Now we need to use our mind and mute our primal instincts.

These instincts are hardwired and can even be passed from one generation to the next, meaning they are hardwired at the genetic level. So whatever deep instincts you have that drive you to the vices we talked about are something that is deep within you. That's one of the reasons the ancients described them as the sins of the flesh. These hardwired instincts are a major force in how and why we do the things we do.

Imaginary Forces

The part of our brain that is responsible for daydreaming and fantasizing is not as wasteful as it sounds. Our entire brain is built on the premise of being able to randomly cook up ideas. This is not inspiration. It is the random mating of ideas. The ability to ask "What if?" is distinctly human and it is distinctly an adult property. Babies don't start off thinking in what-if terms; they randomly do things, and then remember the outcome. The advanced ability to infer and predict outcomes is a trait that sets us apart from other species. Other animals do have the ability to pose what-ifs but to a significantly lesser degree.

The ability to imagine also grows with experience. The more experience we accumulate, the more acute our sense to predict outcomes, and we eventually form guardrails to how we should or shouldn't do things.

When we imagine performing any of the instincts that are deep within us, we are able to imagine the outcome and that in turn prevents us from doing it, but it none-the-less pops up in our head whether we want it or not. It doesn't make us evil; it makes us what we are - human.

Right and Wrong

If you truly want to achieve success, you need to stop thinking in binary terms of right and wrong. In reality, the truth of the matter is that there is no right and wrong, there only is what is. If you think in terms of right and wrong, it was fine while it lasted, but it's time to move on. As children and young adults, we needed the guard rails of right and wrong to keep us safe. They are like training wheels on a kid's bike. But at some point, those training wheels go from being a useful aid to being a useless impediment and need to be discarded. In the same way, your notions of right and wrong got you through adolescence but it's time to move on.

Your notions of right and wrong need to be replaced by the understanding of the consequences of your actions. But to be able to develop your sense of consequence you need to part from your sense of right and wrong first. There is a gap of faith that you must traverse. Once you do, then you are forced to consider and weigh your actions and use your imagination to predict outcomes.

As your sense of consequence develops and your ability to imagine and predict outcomes becomes refined, you begin to understand the value of logic and reasoning. As you develop your powers of reasoning, you start to seek answers to why things result in the way they do and why they can't be something else. The Serpent in George Bernard Shaw's Back to Methuselah says it perfectly, "You see things; and you say, 'Why?' But I dream things that never were; and I say, 'Why not?'" Moving away from right and wrong opens up your mind to this sort of maturity and this sort of power.

That sort of facility in your mind is a prerequisite to grappling with success. You can't be a success unless you are a force that changes and improves on things and you can't do that if you are willing to embrace the status quo, stay within the guardrails, and only ask why but never ask why not.

Takeaway

The important takeaway in all this is that there are three areas of your life that govern your actions when you are on the success path. The first is your feelings (we talked about that as your primal instincts - they come to you as feelings more than as thoughts). The second is your thoughts (these are the things that you cogitate, contemplate, and recall). Finally, there is your inspiration (this is what you get in touch with when you meditate and the content of your inspiration is the pool of the universe)

Inspiration. Feelings. Thoughts. Action.

***

Chapter 2 Dominant Personality

Not all of us are alike. We can certainly categorize people into different traits based on demographics, habits, education, and more, but in reality, every single person is unique in terms of character, motivation, strengths, and weaknesses.

From a functional perspective, one way to categorize the population would be to divide them based on dominant personalities. We look at which area defines their actions, whether it's emotional responses, intellectual responses, or inspired responses. From there we can see how discipline comes into play to be able to move the meter away from actions that are ultimately detrimental and counterproductive to leading and living a life that is ultimately successful.

In the last chapter, we learned that there are three different forces that guide our movement through life. The first is feeling - what are essentially our primal instincts that drive us. They come to us as feelings.

The second is the result of cogitation, reasoning, and memory and we label these as thought.

Finally, we have inspiration that comes to us from the energies of the universe. Many people seem to think that inspiration comes from the mind and that it is some subset of the cognitive process. It's not. Imagination and fantasy is a subset of mental cogitation, but true inspiration is not.

All of us have these three attributes to some degree, especially the first two, thoughts and feelings. Some people are more in tune with their feelings and are labeled emotional, irrational, or romantics. Others are more in tune with thoughts and are described as intelligent, rational, or logical.

Then there are those who go beyond all that and you find them a cut above everyone else. We refer to these people as dreamers. These are like the Isaac Asimovs of the world, dreaming of things that no mind can see until it is up against their nose. These people are truly inspired about what comes next in this physical world and they somehow seem to have the natural gift of being able to tap into the energies of the universe.

Then there is the fourth kind. The kind that has not only brought about the ability to use their mind, their body, and their inspiration, they have even been able to align them in such a way that the three are seamless and highly effective. These are the enlightened among us. In time, the un-illuminated tend to worship these enlightened creatures because their powers - the powers that flow from uniting and aligning mind, body, and spirit, seem omnipotent and omniscient - and it's not because they know so much or have facts at their fingertips, but because their understanding of things is fluid and inspired.

Actions and Reactions

Depending on which category you fall into, will dictate how you act, and how you react. Successful people have their actions down to an art and their reactions are consistent with their desires.

How you act says a lot about how you want people to see you. How you react says a lot about who you really are. Your best bet to get on the path to success is to be able to align the two.

How a person acts can be very different from how a person reacts. Actions usually are based on cogent, collected, and rational thoughts taking numerous factors into consideration. Reactions are usually based on mindsets and habits. If a person has a mindset that is typically negative, then the reaction to the stimuli would most likely be negative. The reason this is important in your quest for discipline is that you need to apply your strength and focus to the part of you that takes control of situations that you seem to not be in control of at this moment.

You need to take a position that you are the purveyor of action and not the slave of reaction. Taking that kind of control is only a matter of discipline. If you conduct an action from no seeming impetus, you may be tempted to call that an action. But remember waking up in the morning may not seem like a reaction to anything, but you wake up at the strike of 6 every morning. What is that if not a habit? So there are times that you must consider that your actions are the result of habits because your actions are in response to something that you are not taking into consideration. All this means is that you need to come to terms with the fact that you are not as independent and alone as you think. Even islands standing way out in the middle of the ocean are really connected to the mainland by the land that sleeps silently beneath the ocean. You must come to terms with the knowledge that we are connected to everything and we are reactionary in almost every way.

Even your inspiration is one that comes from the energy of the universe that you attracted by virtue of who you are. Change who you are and you will change what you attract. It's that simple.

Not only does attraction work for the things that you want to succeed in, but attraction can also change the kind of person you can be to attract different things. It's all a matter of the three parts of you - your soul, your mind, and your body. Who you become, what you succeed in, and what you eventually become great at is the result of the three parts of you aligning their forces.

***

Chapter 3 Purpose

Too many books and misguided notions of deities have compounded man's misunderstanding of purpose. It has come to take on a role that presupposes a reason for the existence of man - meaning, we are taught to think that there is a grand purpose and that is why we are created - to fulfill that purpose. It's like creating a wrench to loosen a bolt. We are not wrenches. Others go on to say that we are created to worship our creator. If so, that makes the power that created us interested in the adulation of the lesser being. Not a very divine quality in my opinion.

So if there is no creator and no purpose, then why are we here?

If you want to take purpose as an empowering force, then you may do so by logically thinking it through. And when you do that, as I and many others have, what you find is that the possibility of a dual-purposed life emerges.

Dual Purpose Life

We don't seem to ever talk about dual purposes, and that's only because we do not ever talk about divergent paths of our two selves. One part of us is driven by the resulting force of two fundamentals in our life. One, being the natural instincts that dictate to us from the very depths of our being; the other, being the societal and communal forces of doing what is acceptable, forced upon us externally. We tend to internalize this in our minds and it is our mind that imposes civility on our potential actions. When these two forces combine there is a resulting vector that charts our path, sometimes forward, sometimes backward, sometimes ebbing and flowing through the course of our earthly lives. If life was just shaped by the resulting effect of these two forces, it would be mundane, uneventful, and unfulfilling. This part of each of us has a simple purpose. There is no great secret here. You can glean the purpose from the things that attract us and the hints that drive this part of us. The purpose of this physical existence is to survive.

The purpose to physically survive transcends time and person. Survival is more about the species and life itself, not so much about the individual. But the single purpose of survival of the species takes on a duality of purpose for the individual. For the species to survive, the individual needs to either live indefinitely or procreate - make a copy of itself in anticipation of future death. So survival and procreation of the individual fulfills the purpose of the species. As far as your body is concerned, that's all you need to do. Those are your marching orders. In order to fulfill this, you do whatever it takes. You adapt and you share resources.

But you can't stop there. You really need to take this further. If you can make that leap, after prolonged observation, you will realize that life itself has a purpose. It's logical and reasonable to come to that conclusion, isn't it? It doesn't matter if it's bug or beast, fish or fawn, all life is headed somewhere, doing something more than just consuming. They are interdependent and together striving for the same grand purpose. That grand purpose is to act as the conduit between the well of divine inspiration and the void of this physical dimension.

The first part of our dual purpose is to stay alive and extend life so that the overall purpose of life itself can manifest. This is the sole purpose of the body, to do whatever is necessary to live and extend life. Every single primal instinct in you is designed to achieve that purpose. The faster you come to realize that and get on board, the better.

The second purpose in this dual-purpose model is based on the part driven by divine inspiration. It is the part of us we touch when we enter a state of meditation. It is the part of us that is the fundamental energy of the universe. The part of us that is divine in nature, but unlike any deity the ancients conjured. It is this energy that unites all of us and keeps us bound as one. This is the same part of us that communicates and draws from the well of the universe. The laws of attraction that have been expounded for some time now and proven time and again, exist simply because we are a part of this universe and that energy within us is not isolated, but rather, an inextricable part of the fabric of the universe's energy matrix.

Whether any purpose is the impetus of our existence, or whether our existence gave rise to our purpose doesn't matter one bit. It's whatever you believe. What matters is that there is a dual purpose and the more we understand them, prioritize them, and get to work, the better we become.

Greatness is Your Purpose

If you want to extract more from yourself than you are currently able to, you will need to understand the very basic nature and purpose of the human condition. You will need to realize, whether you subscribe to the theory of evolution or the theology of creationism, the one truth that survives both arguments is that we have a purpose, and its basis is not in silly notions. Our purpose is matched perfectly to the states of our being. Our physical body is pre-purposed to survive, while our divine purpose of existence is to pursue greatness.

So the choice is yours. What do you want to do? Do you want to live up to your divine purpose and let your body keep going, or do you want to give in to the physical purpose and just be a vassal for a hollow existence?

Every single one of us is born to take part in this greatness. Every single one of us can be great and can be divine in stature. But the inability to shake off the robe of familiarity and the veil of ignorance stops 99.9% of human beings from fully manifesting the greatness that is within them.

Is Greatness Not for Everyone?

There are some who argue, unsuccessfully, that not everyone can be great. That's not true. They think that if everyone is great, who is going to do the menial tasks that could never add up to greatness. Good question, but it's a fallacy. If you stick to what you know and do not want to leap forward and adapt, then you are going to go extinct. Asking this question is like the person who asked why we need the patent office since everything that needs to be invented has already been invented. Of course, that joke was back in 1899, and since then, you must agree, the human mind has come up with more than we could have imagined. To the uninspired vassal, we seem to always live at the edge of all possibilities. But to the inspired mind, and the willing back, there is so much more that can be done and we need all hands on deck.

We can all be great and leave the menial tasks to robots, machines, and computers.

Unfortunately, the status quo is something we are generally comfortable with. Take for instance the coal industry that is based on outdated technology. Those who work in that industry adamantly want to keep doing what they are doing and continue working the subterranean mines to extract the supply of coal. This method of energy extraction is out of date and dangerous for those in the mines, and by extension, dangerous to the population at large due to pollution. But yet they don't see it because they are not willing to jump to something other than what they are used to. While they do that, they fail to see that technology has already solved the energy extraction problem that existed when coal driven energy generation was developed.

The coal miners are the example of a class of jobs that are going extinct with the development of new technology, and all the miners have to do is adapt to the changing conditions. Adapting is hard but if you have the will, you can. You just have to get off your laurels and do it. But societal forces make this difficult.

Are you in a situation that's similar? Are you unwilling to jump forward because you are satisfied where you are right now? Success will never grace your doorstep if all you want to do is hold on to what only feeds your body's purpose but not your divine purpose.

What has this got to do with the ability to be great and how someone must be left to do the menial tasks? Who is going to do the menial tasks that could never add up to greatness? The answer is that if we are willing to let go of what is comfortable and what is familiar and embrace what is new, if we are willing to let the raft remain at the river while we trek forward, then we can leave the menial tasks to technology while we, each and every one of us, develop a new frontier. Imagine an economy where every single person is successful at doing more; where everyone is not living a hollow existence. It is possible, but you don't have to worry about everyone, you just have to worry about you. Can you step up to greatness?

Chapter 4 An Introduction to Discipline

There are three kinds of discipline to understand. Each is defined by the situation it is subjected to, and the outcome that is desired. In sequence, they are introduced below.

Filial Discipline

Filial discipline is the core of our introduction, understanding and eventual perspective on the subject. We are first introduced to this concept by means of a word that really means obedience. As children, we heard the term often, especially in strict households or from strict school masters. After repeated exposure to the term, especially in less than comfortable circumstances, we slowly begin to form a visceral understanding of the word.

There are two problems that arise from this early introduction to the word and the meaning behind it. Most parents, if they know what discipline means, wield it with good intention, alerting the child to his or her inability to obey a command. Because the commands issued to children are usually to protect or guide them, it is necessary that the commands are followed explicitly and remembered for future use.

Filial discipline is outgrown, or at least it should be. Filial discipline should not be transferred to other actors that pass in a person's life. It should not be transferred to spouses or friends. Filial discipline has a finite lifespan and is personal.

Under the hood, you will find that filial discipline works well as an inverse function of age, bond, self-confidence, and parental stature. The younger the child, the higher levels of discipline they display - provided they understand the instruction to begin with. They are obedient and listen to instructions well enough to remember them over a reasonable span of time. When there is a strong bond between parents and children, there is a higher level of obligation in the child and the desire to please the parents.

Kids with high levels of self-confidence are not usually possessed by the discipline of performing what their parents tell them; they are seemed to have minimal discipline. That's not because they bond any less with their parents but because they are very independent in thought. They find motivation in doing what their hearts dictate. There is a lot of potential in these children, but they still need to be taught discipline so that when the time comes they would be able to transfer the discipline to their conscious thought and rationale. Teaching discipline to children is a good practice so that they learn to understand how to use it in moments of impulse.

Societal Discipline

Societal discipline is about conforming to and obeying hard or soft rules that are set within the community. They include formal laws set by the competent jurisdictions of your location. For instance, wherever you stand at this moment, your rights and prohibitions are the subject of the laws governed by the municipality, state, and country that you are in. Your discipline is required so that you follow those laws. For instance, you may come from a country that prohibits alcohol consumption even in moderate amounts during social gatherings. You may not be used to this and not see the harm, but you need the discipline to be able to refrain from breaking those laws, right or wrong in your judgment, to avoid negative consequences in the immediate future.

The same rationale goes for norms and practices of the region you are in. There may not be hard and fast laws that compel you to do things, but you face societal pressure to conform and so your discipline will override your urge to go against them.

Personal Discipline

Earlier on, we saw that there is a constant battle that goes on between our thoughts and feelings. The thoughts generated in our head and the feelings generated by our instinct can sometimes be at odds with each other and we are left in a state of confusion of what to go after. It can either bring us to a grinding halt, or it can confuse us into inaction.

At times, the feelings in us can be so overwhelming that we are intellectually incapacitated and find that we end up acting on our feeling more than on our logical reasoning. This is where discipline is needed.

Discipline is needed to override the feeling to do something that can be extremely compelling. The tools at the disposal of primal instincts are extremely powerful. The can create a hunger in you to do something and reward you with bliss once you have done it. Your thoughts and reasoning, on the other hand, can do no such thing. There is no carrot and stick mechanism in the cerebral actions that you take. So if you decide, after weighing all the research, to quit smoking, it is your cerebral mind that is making the choice; your body, on the other hand, is going to go into revolt.

We make promises to ourselves all the time, but the consequence of not keeping them up is almost nonexistent. There a feeling of guilt in some situations, but it's never as compelling as the way the body torments you in the wake of not complying with its bidding. There is also no pleasure from the cerebral instructions when they are done, as there would be when you accomplish what the body makes you do; you don't really get the same tangible rewards you get when you do the body's bidding.

Carrot and Stick

The hunger and reward system of the body is an innate system, but the mind's system of compelling action from desire is discipline. For you to be able to do what needs to be done, you need to be able to instill a new brand of discipline. If you were taught discipline as a child then it is usually easier for you to be able to transfer that discipline to your cerebral side. Because the discipline is just a way of being able to conquer your body's reward and hunger system.

In many people, this is a harsh reality and it is the key deficiency in people who are unsuccessful.

We are subject to a simple matrix. On one axis we are influenced by the carrot and the stick - reward and punishment. On the other axis, we are influenced by internal and external forces. On the third axis, we are influenced by what we believe and what we are forced to do. Where we are at any given moment in time is a function of all three axes. It's like a three-dimensional grid that gives x, y and z coordinates. Once we get to the point that we are affixed to, we fall in love with it and are afraid to move away from it because the unknown seems more daunting than whatever we are facing at the moment. But the one single factor that you can muster to move you from your current location to a higher existence is discipline.

The Arc of Discipline

Whether you have discipline is something only you can tell for certain. If a person were to observe you for some period of time, they could start to have a sense of whether you possess any amount of it, but the best person to always be the judge of that is yourself. You need to take a long hard look and understand if you have what it takes to compel yourself to do what it takes when it is required, not when you are forced by circumstances to do it.

There are tons of people, who when they are put in a corner, can suddenly transform and turn things around. Do you realize that that is a matter of discipline - not just motivation? Motivation is designed to parallel or to boost discipline. For those who do not need a lot of motivation, that goes to show that you have high levels of discipline. When you have low levels of discipline, you need to be able to find the external motivation, either positive motivation that pulls you to success or negative motivation that pushes you from the fear of consequences. Either way, that's not the best way for you to develop discipline.

If you have zero discipline, the picture your life would paint is one where all your actions are dictated by your binary instincts. You will only do the things that your body commands and then rewards when it is done. You will be the kind of person that is easily addicted to substances – smoking, alcohol, or drugs, or you are easily attracted to gambling and other vices that have a high payoff upon execution. Once in, without discipline, the downward spiral quickens and tightens until your life is unrecognizable and depleted.

On the other hand, a full deck of discipline means that you can basically command anything into existence. You can command, sitting on the side of your cerebral center, anything that you think to be logical and reasonable and your body will acquiesce and fall in line. You will be like a Vulcan from Star Trek.

Most of us fall within the standard deviation of that spectrum, neither on one extreme nor the other and always with room to improve. Even if you are fairly successful, there are ways and there is a need to be able to increase your level of discipline.

The Importance of Discipline

Whether we are adequately inspired, or we are following someone else's playbook, the ability to take what we plan and execute it into action is the reason we need discipline. Without it, all we ever desire and hope for will remain a dream.

The importance of discipline can never be overstated and it is the most important thing one needs to develop. Even if you are able to meditate for better inspiration, follow the rules of failing and getting up, learning in every way you can what steps you need to take, all those won't matter if you can't invoke the discipline you need to actually put your back into it and get some skin into the game.

The Insidious Nature of Indiscipline

It is said that we all suffer one of two kinds of pain. We either suffer the pain of discipline or the pain of never seeing the goal accomplished. The problem with indiscipline is that it becomes a habit and that habit can feed off of itself. When you quit something because your body is not willing, you are rewarded when you stop. Why are you rewarded? Because the body has the power to reward you when you do something it wants. When your body is not interested in getting off its laurels to get something done, it will reward you when you comply. When you comply once too often, you find that you will start many things in life, and then quit, and still feel good about yourself.

There is no other way to put it, you have, at this point become a serial loser.

Why Does the Body Not Want to Act?

The foremost economist you know is no further than the core of your body's internal resource management system. It is always calculating a number of resources it needs to apply to an act and if it is able to get more back than what it puts in.

If your body knows that a banana will give it 100 calories, and that banana is located 2 miles away, since it takes your body 100 calories to walk one mile, those two miles you have to walk will cost you two hundred calories. Your body realizes that this is not worth the effort. On the other hand, it the banana was just a few steps away, it will go for it, without hesitation. Of course, this is a very simplistic example of how corporal economics works, but the reality is not too far away. It actually works by ascribing a value to something based on experience and how much effort it needs to expend and how much risk there is in getting the reward, and how much risk there is in getting to the prize. Once it calculates everything, it rewards your body for going after it or rewards your body to stay put.

The body will not act if it thinks that the effort is not worth it. So, instead of completely obviating what your body is telling you to do, you need to look at what its concerns are. It is just another factor that your logical mind can take into consideration. But once it does and your mind still feels that the prize is worth the effort, then overriding the body's reluctance is what discipline is about.

You can do that in one of two general ways. You can either brute force your way around it, or you can teach it, and over time your discipline becomes visceral.

***

Chapter 5 Overcoming Resistance to Action

Before it becomes a habit, and before this habit fights your cerebral decisions tooth and nail, the way you overcome resistance to action is different from when you have to deal with it after it becomes a habit.

There are three ways you can pull this off before it is habitual. The first is you play the same game your body is playing. You play the reward and punishment system. Whenever you decide to do something and the body complies, reward it when the job is successfully completed. By doing this, you are associating the task with something the body can expect. It is realigning its cost-reward matrix, and over time, it starts to actually realize the benefit of doing what you have decided is actually even more rewarding in the long term than just the reward you give it. This is not a good idea with kids; the need for rewards to comply can get out of hand.

The second way is to brute force it and psych yourself into not listening to any dissent from any part of you about doing what you have to do. There is a problem with doing this though, and it will most likely make you robotic in your approach and leave out any room for constant evaluation of your current circumstance. This is dangerous because it does not give you any room to reevaluate in the event your initial assumptions have changed and the outcome is different.

The third way for you to overcome resistance is to use discipline. Incorporating discipline into the process is the best option of the three. As mentioned in the last part of chapter 3, there are two ways you can invoke discipline. The first is to be able to practice discipline in other areas of your life. This is how discipline can become visceral. The second is for you to be able to understand how discipline feels and embrace it. Both of these strategies are two sides of the same coin and you can invoke it by doing a few exercises for short periods of time.

You must understand that discipline is not a one-off thing that you look at one day when you are interested in becoming successful, then you go on and do something else. Discipline is a state and a lifestyle, not a punishment. Discipline is rewarding in the long run but never gratifying in the short term. Discipline is the state that all successful people in the world have invoked to get to where they are. You cannot avoid discipline if you want to be able to succeed.

If you can remember this and do whatever it takes to get disciplined without the need for excessive external motivation, then you are about to become successful beyond your wildest dreams.

Let's put aside our divine potential for the moment. Let's just look at resolving the battle between our primal instinct and our civilized and intellectual center. Without being able to do this, getting to the point where we can ignite our actions with cosmic flames is out of the question.

As you've read, you have a raging battle between your hard coded instincts and your civilized mind. It's a fight that needs settling and it can only be done with the development of discipline. Without discipline you will not be able to execute what you have decided is the best course of action for any given situation or when you chose which side wins in a dispute. That will slowly degrade into becoming chaos, because after a few times of not executing the proper course of action, you will eventually give up on even trying.

***

Chapter 6 Face to Face With Discipline

Scour the internet all you want, and the proper definition of discipline will still elude you. It did me. The only place I could find it was within myself, and across the long unrelated books on philosophy that were milestones of the ages.

Simple textbook definitions and dictionary blurbs did nothing to truly elaborate on a concept that has such vast implications and such power to change the course of one's life. What you are in search of is the essence of a power to withstand an internal force that grips everyone in one way or another. What you need to find is the antidote to the poison of the flesh. What you need to identify is the shield against the arrows of the devil himself.

That is what discipline is, in essence. It is the shield, it is the antidote, and it is the power to withstand. At its truest, discipline covers a wide spectrum of opposing forces and tips the balance in the direction of a logical and well-reasoned solution.

Whether you realize it or not, discipline is a cognitive tool, unlike hunger and pain, which are tools of the body. But the thing you need to wrap your mind around is that discipline can even be brought to bear in the way you think as well.

For example, in people who are inherently and psychologically negative - the kind of people who would think that something lurks behind a blue-skied, bright sunny day, are those who have not brought any discipline to the mind and so the mind has degenerated to the point that it is always on heightened caution and negative in its outlook. In short, you can discipline your mind, not just your body or your instincts.

Thoughts

There are two broad classes of thoughts. Thoughts that occur randomly are the first kind. The second are thoughts that you will into existence. You read a book and think about the content of the book, for instance. Each of the two has positive potential and both have negative potential as well. You have the ability to control both.

If you are the over-cautious kind, it is very likely that you develop negative thoughts over time. Once you start to develop them and those negative thoughts come to fruition, you reward them for being right and for saving you from possible harm. This empowers negative thoughts. When the negative thoughts are empowered, you begin to form strong negative mindsets and from there you end up shading all things that you are exposed to.

All your actions are driven by thoughts. Whether they are fresh thoughts or thought patterns that become habits, your actions can't happen without them being formed as a thought. Thoughts lead to actions. Actions lead to consequences. Consequences are either beneficial or destructive and consequences either manifest in the short term or over a long horizon. Consequences that are in the short-term form habits faster, consequences that manifest in the long term form habits, slower or not at all.

When you look at this chain of events, you start to understand that your thoughts, whether willed or random have an impact on your life and you must find a way to control your thoughts to be able to take control of your life.

This is the first and most important kind of discipline - the discipline of thinking. There are positive ways of looking at things just as there are negative ways of looking at things. The worst state to be in is the state that fosters negative thoughts; the state that promotes excess caution and distrust.

The middle of the road is the state of positive thoughts. In many scenarios, it is advised that people have positive thoughts. Positive thoughts may be great for the short term but they are not practical and do not do anything to advance your ability to be disciplined or successful. Seeing things positively and not as they are can get you in trouble. It also doesn't do anything to be able to see the truth.

What you really need is the third option. You need to be able to see things for what they are. You need to be pragmatic so that your mind is not influenced one way or the other before it has a chance to analyze the data and see things for what they are. Being happy is often confused with being positive. But being positive is not about how you analyze things; being positive comes at a much higher level.

Being positive is applied at a higher plain. It is about knowing that whatever truth you are faced with, you can make it into to a position that is advantageous for you. You just need to have the discipline to think pragmatically about all things.

This brings us to your natural state of mind. Your natural state of mind should be one that is happy because you know two things. You know whatever you are faced with, you will be able to see things as they are and you can garner significant safety from that because when you see things as they are, you will be able to fix anything. Once you can control your thoughts to be pragmatic with the aid of discipline, you then need to look at how that translates in the real world.

Actions

Actions come from thoughts, but there is a gap. Not all thoughts translate to actions, and not all thoughts should translate to actions. You need to have the discipline to apply to which thought translates to action. This is your second step in discipline. It's a different kind of discipline with a different consequence profile.

Once you discipline your mind to generate the kinds of thoughts that are beneficial to you in the short and long term, you are now in a position to put them into action. Converting thoughts to actions is almost as hard as thinking about the right things. You need to be able to apply the energy necessary to be able to pull off what your thought has decided to do. This takes resolve. It also takes discipline to be able to do it constantly and consistently.

Discipline Flows from Focus

The best way to be able to keep your body doing what your mind has decided is to keep your mental focus constant. Most of us decide to do something, pass the instruction along, and allow our minds to move on to the next thing. That's where the problem starts. Because for the body to be under the control of the mind, the mind needs to be constantly watching. If you allow your mind to step away, your body is going to disregard its instructions and your mind won't be there to compel it back in line.

***

Chapter 7 How to Invoke Discipline

By this point, you already get the importance of discipline. In fact, what you are probably expecting is to be able to learn a few tips and tricks to be able to bring discipline to bear on your thoughts and actions. That's exactly what we are going to do right now. We are going to look at ways to bring it online and become super effective at accomplishing what you need to accomplish to become successful and put yourself on the road to greatness.

Focus

To be able to convert thought to action you need to be able to keep your mind focused on what you are doing. The moment you take your mind off of something you can't really expect your body to be able to do it on its own. You know why? Because the economics of energy kicks in and the body knows that it can't do what the mind can. The moment the body is in charge of the task that is supposed to be in the mind's realm, the body gives in and throws in the towel and goes about doing something else. And the body is right; you are not lazy or useless, you are just not focused. Your inability to focus could be that you are stressed over the outcome and that causes your mental state to be something other than what it needs to be to get the job done.

Focus is important because as long as your mind is involved in what you have decided to do, then the only thing left is for your body to do and your mind to reassure it that all is well. That's the extent of the discipline you need. You really just need to be present. Once you are present, the body will fall in line. This is the key to being mindful. Being mindful allows you to stay focused, and staying focused allows you to stay in control and remain disciplined.

Discipline is as easy as keeping your mind focused on what you are doing, and you can do that by being pragmatic and following the first instruction. Being mindful is the first path to invoking discipline.

There is a second path, and the second path is something that you were taught if you were one of those people who went to military school or boarding school. The way to enforce discipline in all your areas is to act it out in everything you do. From the way you wake up to the way to eat your lunch to the way you get to sleep at night, if you invoke and enforce discipline, it will manifest in other areas of your life as well. From that, it will flow into the areas of your life where cerebral thought opposes primal instinct, and what feels good to do is no longer as important as what needs to be done.

There is a simple exercise you can do to see how willful action can invoke an inward state. The next time you are sad, force yourself to physically laugh. Do that a few times and you will find that you are suddenly less upset or less unhappy. The same thing goes for the way you stand. If you are down in the dumps and you are slouched over, instead of trying to make yourself feel happy and stand brisk, force yourself to stand brisk and you will find that you will get happy. The inward grace can dictate your outward action, just as much as your outward action can be dictated by your inward grace.

Thoughts and acts are inextricably connected. And discipline is not the only way they connect. You can also connect them through your sheer will and change how you feel. You can force discipline without actually forcing it. The way you pull this off is to be able to set a certain goal, a small one is fine. And go out and pay attention to it until it is one. Do it well and do it with total conviction, never once leaving it to automation or mindlessness.

For this to take hold, you need to apply this to all things. From arising in the morning, when you first open your eyes at the sound of the alarm, you need to bring your mind online. The reason people who hit the snooze button do so is because their brain is not in gear yet. The same thing happens to people who are intoxicated or who are so tired their body is up but their mind is absent. To be able to be disciplined simply means to be able to engage your mind to what you have instructed your body to do.

And this, just like anything else, takes lots of practice. The more you practice this, the more you will be able to apply your mind to what you are doing without giving it a second thought.

Energy Economics

Earlier in the book, we talked about the allocation of energy and how the mind weighed one action against how much energy it has to expend to how much utility it gets in return. The example was simplistic but you get an idea of what is at play here. There are a few more factors that you need to take into account to be able to get that model to approximate the real deal.

Not only does the mind calculate the effort expended and the return that is possible, it also applies a probabilistic score to the return. It simply looks at how probable the outcome of the effort will be. If it is a 100% outcome, then all systems are go. But if the mind calculates that the probability is not worth the effort, then it rewards the body to be lazy and wait for the next opportunity.

Because of this, there is one thing that you have to now change in your mind if you want to be successful.

You must adopt the do or die attitude. Don't worry, you are not really going to die. But in saying that you are committing to the point that you disregard calamity and throw caution to the wind, you are saying that nothing matters to you more that achieving consistent success and greatness. You are either going to make something of yourself or you are going to die trying.

Why do we put it in these terms? Why do we make it sound so terminal? Well, you have to because the entire point of the body's economics is to go on living. Your body is tasked with living life; it's not tasked with living a successful life. Living life is the body's prerogative, being successful is the soul's.

We put it in these terms so that your body changes its economic principles and it realizes at a fundamental level that discipline towards action and success is better than failure or doing nothing. It is designed to make you realize that you are better off trying hard and in the event, you exceed your ability and perish, that's fine too. You have to make it, or living a hollow life without success and achievement is a life is not worth living.

The more you think in these terms, the more you will notice that your behavior changes over time. Have you ever watched people who are willing to jump off cliffs, take risks, go around the world in a balloon? Feats that some of you think are just absolutely crazy?

Well, the fundamental difference between them and you is that they have adopted the do-or-die attitude and to them, success and achievement are more worthy than a life of sedentary boredom and lack of accomplishment. Achievement, to them, is a high.

You have managed to change your thoughts at this point, and you have learned to change your actions. You use those to change your behavior and create a habit of doing that. Once you do, your ability to succeed increases. The more you attempt something and the more you achieve, your body starts to realize that the probability of success is a lot higher and it too begins to recoil less.

Behavioral Change

When you start to change your behavior, you will notice that success is more easily attained. Using the term 'easy' here is not meant to diminish the fact that your effort is still a necessity, but rather, the battle between the desire to accomplish and the body's inability to move, begin to reconcile. You start to see that movement is in itself a way of getting things done and changing your fortune. It is the tool of the successful and the power of the mighty.

***

Chapter 8 Theory vs. Practice

Just understanding the theory of discipline is not nearly enough to get it to work for you. You need to put it to practice, and to do that there are a couple of exercises you can do to get your mind and body into strict adherence to discipline. Most of the time discipline is taught in environments of pain and suffering.

Let's start with a few things you can do to get your discipline into high gear. We don't assume that you have any form of discipline and it doesn't matter if you have some or you have none. Either way, you can get on this short program and build your fortitude and your discipline to the point that you can do whatever it takes to get the outcome you envision.

Remember, to get your body into action on something and dictate the outcome, you need to be in a position where you are constantly in focus and you are able to take charge.

Exercises

There are two exercises you can do to enhance your ability to be disciplined. They are small steps in the beginning and eventually can change your entire way of approaching life. Since discipline is about taking control of your body's will on your actions, the best way to tame it is to fast.

The biggest tool that the body has on you can be the fear of doing something. For instance, most people have the fear that if they go hungry for a day or two, they will die. For most people who are in healthy condition and have a few pounds to spare, that is not true in any shape or form. Most people, especially those who are overweight can probably go on fasting for at least five or six days (from personal experience) without anything adverse happening.

The longest I have fasted is seven days. In that time, all I had was water to remain hydrated, and I found out many things about the way my body tries to control my actions. I found that the greatest tool it has against my will is the tool of fear. The body has the ability to ignite anxiety and panic and that is enough to sow seeds of doubt and dissension in the brain. Understanding the source of those fears, and understanding the profile of how you feel goes a long way in arresting the negative feelings the body throws at you when it does not want to do what you ask.

I have found that there are two key aspects of life that hyper successful people understand thoroughly. The first is that they realize meditation (which we cover in another book in the series) is key to success. The second is that they find out that denying your senses and keeping sharp plays a huge role in who you are and how well you can do things.

This is where fasting comes into play.

Fasting

Contrary to popular belief, fasting is not about piety. Fasting is about self-discipline and the ability to enhance your strength over being enslaved by the will of the body. The body is not trying to make you lose the game, the body is just doing what it has to do. It is up to you to keep that in check. One way to do that is to teach the body that its instincts of eating and foraging and fasting have changed from the genesis of life to now.

The body can easily fast, and survive, but the body doesn't know that and that creates a sense of fear and panic in the event of a fasting exercise. When you ride over the desire to eat and show the body that you can still come out okay at the end of it, you teach the body how to win. You know that saying, whatever doesn't kill you only makes you stronger. Well, it applies here as well. Because the body thinks if it skips a meal it's starving - not true. The body thinks that if it skips two or three meals, it's at the point of getting ill, and possibly fainting or dying - also not true. So the only way to show it is to actually do it.

When you fast for two days, you will notice that the desire to eat is as much a desire to fulfill a habit, as it is a desire to be rewarded by satiety for eating and for the ability for the body to accumulate nutrition and energy. But in today's world, we all eat more than we need to and there are plenty of stores that the body can hold on to.

When you are at the gym and you are trying to build yourself up, your body throws everything it has at you from making you feel tired to making the pain almost intolerable. I have found the best way to drown all those out is to invoke mindfulness and turn away from the dissent that your body is screaming. When you are mindful, you are able to face away from the pain; you will start to realize that mindfulness empowers your mind over your body. It is literally a case of mind over matter. In a nutshell, that's exactly what discipline is. When you take the mindfulness route to discipline, what you find is that you are in control and when the time comes that you need to maneuver, you have the ability to do so without breaking your fortitude or resolve.

Muscle Building

Just to get it straight, this is not about buffing up or working out. Weight lifting/push-ups and strength training are great ways to make the lack of discipline apparent and locate the source of your deficiency. Pushing one more time or lifting one more time takes a lot of discipline when your body is screaming out in pain. The more you can do that, the more you will learn how to recognize the voice of dissent and empower the will to succeed. If you can't get to the gym, that's fine, do push-ups. Be religious about it. Do it two to three times a day. When Muhammad Ali was asked how many push-ups he does, he said that he didn't count because it didn't matter. What mattered, he said, was how many time he pushed back against the pain. The number he was busy counting was, "One More".

Fasting and weight lifting are super activities that will build your resistance to resistance. Each time you push your body you are subconsciously learning how to control it and it is learning who is in charge.

One great advantage in using fasting and strength training is that you get to keep it to yourself. You don't need a guru to teach you how to fast, and you don't need a trainer to teach you how to lift weights or do push-ups. You just do them.

When I fasted for seven days straight with only water to keep me hydrated, I worked out six of those seven days. Note, I am not advocating that you do the same. I am merely sharing with you my personal experience.

I felt fine the first day of fasting, and the workout was effortless. I don't know how many pushups I did in total because I didn't count the ones that didn't hurt. But of the ones that did hurt, I was able to do sixty the first day.

The second day's fast was a little annoying because my mind was unrelenting in its push to get me to eat. When I worked out that day, I hit seventy push-ups but at the end of the day, I felt sick.

I woke up the third day in pain. My muscles hurt, each one hurling the most violent of curses at my decision to seemingly punish my body. I tried everything but it was total chaos inside. I continued to fast, but my vision was a little blurry, my head was pounding some serious migraine and I was in a terrible mood. It was my breaking point and I came face to face with what resolve looks like and what the demons opposing that resolve were. My biggest challenge was getting my mind to push my body. I decided that I was going to do this or die trying. (Yes, a little melodramatic, I know, but that's the kind of battle you have to wage)

On the fourth day, I decided to meditate. I started the morning with a walk and push-ups, which I was able to get to eighty-two. My muscles stopped responding at 83. I used the push-ups to get me to get focused and used the breathing to get into a state of mindfulness. I launched from there into meditation and kept my mind in check. It was like erecting a force field around an explosion. It kept my mind contained and channeled my energy instead of allowing it to go in every direction.

The rest of the day was stable. My cravings for food had stopped but I was still weak. Doctors later told me that it was just the gap before my body's metabolic pathways switched to burning energy that was in storage. I continued my work out and my push-ups reached 85 before I stopped. The rest of the day seemed clearer than the day before.

On the sixth day, I continued meditation, and took my work out further. Was able to walk a couple of times around the block and felt a strange sense of clarity and empowerment. My push-ups reached 103 before I stopped. My mind was clear. My resolve was razor sharp and the demons had retreated to a whisper.

I slept for four hours that night, waking up on my own without the aid of an alarm. I rose fresh. Not a sound was stirring in me. There was a sense of peace, but not the kind of peace that is relaxed. It was a focused sense of ability.

While it may sound like a pamphlet advocating fasting, it's not. Because all that would not have been possible if I was not able to stand up to the screaming voices in me unanimously deriding me for inflicting the suffering. It was discipline that pushed me across. It can do the same for you.

***

Conclusion

There are many ways we can bring discipline to bear in our lives. Everything from waking up at a certain time of the morning, to working out at a certain level of output. These are mere examples of simple exercises in discipline. But the discipline we all need to be able to be successful consistently is one of a different pedigree.

The discipline we need here is one that arrests the vagrancies of the mind and halts the primal instincts of the body, all in an effort to fine-tune the mind and body to be able to take the inspiration of the soul and make it a reality. That is no small feat. If you don't think so, just ask the Wright Brothers. Ask Thomas Edison, Ask Linus Pauling. The amount of discipline one needs to be able to make things that no one else sees and to be able to hold that vision in your head till your hands can make it a reality is what legends are made of.

When it all comes down to it, no matter how you cut it, discipline is intangible, but it has significant tangible results. Discipline is the force of the mind that makes sure that you do what you say you're going to do. And the secret to doing it is simple. All you have to do is keep your mind fixed on your body that is doing the work. As long as your mind is engaged, your body is never going to say no. On the other hand, if you let your mind drift, your body is going to want to go out and play.

In the first book, you looked at Failing Your Way to Success. It is easier said than done. The one missing element required to fail and learn, and to do that consistently, is the discipline to pick yourself up and do it again, and again, and again - against all the opposing forces and all daunting odds. It is difficult, not only to fight your body's resistance but to fight the ego that is getting bruised by the constant avalanche of naysayers telling you that you are overreaching and that you should just take what you have got and go home before you lose everything.

It's hard to move the needle of progress when, in the middle of giving it your all, your family is in the throes of a difficult life and intermittent hunger. It's hard. No doubt. It's easy for a guy to sit in a comfortable chair writing words of grand plans and telling you to go out and push through the pain. But I am not that guy.

I've been in the belly of the beast. I have intimate knowledge of the pain you must endure to come out the other end, scathed, burned, and bruised but alive and better for it. Calm winds do not a good sailor make. So you should tell the winds to bring it on. That's what I did.

The five elements that came together in my life to extract diamonds from coal are laid out across these five books on Success. Different people I speak to have challenges in one or more of the elements. The most common is the subject of this book - discipline. But the one thing that you need to conquer at the beginning of any journey, especially when you are about to get underway to launch your attempt at success is the cruelest adversary of all - momentum. Believe it or not, even the destitute are kept down by momentum. The only thing that will help you to free those chains is discipline. So when I tell you that one element that will make it all fall into place and happen for you is discipline - you better believe it.

***

Epilogue

Do not confuse success with achievement. Everyone makes that mistake. We all know how to achieve. We set a goal, we do it, and we achieve it. Not a big deal, we learned to do that in kindergarten. We all have achievements to speak of, in the past, and we can all build on them. But being a success, which is very different from just succeeding at something or achieving something, is serious business.

It requires the desire to do something phenomenal. It requires the inspiration of the universe that we attract and know how to recognize. It requires the search for knowledge and the buildup of ability to make real. It requires the discipline to pursue and to transform from intangible plans and ideas into workable and effective reality.

You can achieve a task by following instructions. But to be successful, you need to tie your mind, body, and soul together in a seamless continuum. You need to be inspired, disciplined, energized, and sharp all at the same time. You need to be proactive. You need to be tireless, and you need to be fearless.

We all want to succeed in life. We are not always sure why we get that desire, but we do. We think success is localized and relevant only over the next quarter or just in our neighborhood or, at best, among our circle of associates. After all that, we go to bed at night wondering where we are in life and how it seems insufficient. On the other hand, we are perfectly content with our weekly sports night, our annual mid-budget vacations, or TV dinners, a mortgaged house and our leased vehicle. We think that's success.

It's not.

What you're doing, does not amount to success until your handiwork has an impact on the world. Unless you are adding to this world something that inspires you and you've worked at bringing it to life and it's now out there making a difference - you're not a success. And as long as you are not a success, you will continue to be rewarded as such. The true reward of success is deep and peaceful contentment. There will always be something missing inside you if you do not make success your life.

Two of the linchpins of success, which you have read time and again in this book, are the ability to be inspired and to do something that can make a difference. You do not need to know it it's going to make a difference when you start; all you need is to make sure you are inspired by it. Let the market worry about itself. But get inspired, now. Learn how to get inspired and then rev that up.

The second is having the discipline to convert inspiration into action and deliverables. In the next book in this Success series, we present the ways to refine the process of being inspired. We take you through the steps of doing it by meditation, mindfulness, and focus.

All that's covered in the next book, Meditate Your Way to Success. In it you will get to understand the reason high achievers advocate meditation. You will learn why meditation is not necessarily religious or spiritual. And you will get to understand how important focus and mindfulness are in their own right and how they set the stage for a path to meditation and the development of constant inspiration.

Between your understanding of discipline and your eventual understanding of meditation and the other areas covered in this series, you will be on your way to being unstoppable.

***

Make sure to check out the rest of the books in this series:

Fail Your Way to Success: The Definitive Guide to Failing Forward and Learning How to Extract the Greatness Within - Why Failing is an Integral Part of Success and Why You Should Never Fear it

https://www.amazon.com/dp/B0738WDK6W

Meditate Your Way to Success: The Definitive Guide to Mindfulness, Focus and Meditation - How Meditation is an Integral Part of Success and Why You Should Get Started Now

https://www.amazon.com/dp/B073ZMCHQJ

Ask Your Way to Success: The Definitive Guide to Success Through Asking - How to Transform Your Life by Learning the Art of Asking

https://www.amazon.com/dp/B074CJPFMH

Believe Your Way to Success: The Definitive Guide to Believing and Your Path to Success How Believing Takes You from Where You are to Where You Want to Be

https://www.amazon.com/dp/B0747N14KF

www.ingramcontent.com/pod-product-compliance
Lightning Source LLC
Chambersburg PA
CBHW021134300426

44113CB00006B/430